AMERICAN GOVERNMENT
Governments Series

Written by Brenda Vance Rollins, Ed. D.

GRADES 5 - 8
Reading Levels 3 - 4

Classroom Complete Press

P.O. Box 19729
San Diego, CA 92159
Tel: 1-800-663-3609 | Fax: 1-800-663-3608
Email: service@classroomcompletepress.com

www.classroomcompletepress.com

ISBN 13: 978-1-55319-343-2
ISBN 10: 1-55319-343-1

© 2007

Permission to Reproduce

Critical Thinking Skills

American Government

Skills For Critical Thinking	Reading Comprehension								
	Section 1	Section 2	Section 3	Section 4	Section 5	Section 6	Section 7	Section 8	Writing Tasks
LEVEL 1 Knowledge									
• List Facts / Details			✓	✓	✓			✓	✓
• Recall Information	✓	✓	✓	✓	✓			✓	✓
• Match	✓	✓		✓	✓	✓	✓	✓	
• Sequence			✓			✓			
• Recognize Validity (T/F)		✓	✓	✓	✓		✓	✓	
LEVEL 2 Comprehension									
• Compare & Contrast		✓		✓					
• Summarize	✓		✓	✓	✓				✓
• State Main Idea			✓		✓		✓		✓
• Describe		✓	✓		✓	✓	✓	✓	✓
LEVEL 3 Application									
• Apply What Is Learned	✓			✓			✓	✓	
• Infer Outcomes							✓		
LEVEL 4 Analysis									
• Draw Conclusions	✓	✓			✓	✓	✓	✓	✓
• Make Inferences		✓			✓	✓	✓		✓
• Identify Cause & Effect						✓			✓
LEVEL 5 Synthesis									
• Predict					✓		✓		✓
• Design		✓						✓	✓
• Create								✓	✓
• Compile Research		✓	✓	✓	✓	✓	✓	✓	✓
LEVEL 6 Evaluation									
• Defend An Opinion							✓		✓
• Make Judgements					✓		✓		✓

Based on Bloom's Taxonomy

Contents

TEACHER GUIDE

STUDENT HANDOUTS

✔ **6 BONUS** Activity Pages! **Additional worksheets for your students**

FREE!

- Go to our website: **www.classroomcompletepress.com/bonus**
- Enter item CC5757
- Enter pass code CC5757D

Assessment Rubric

American Government

Student's Name: _____ Assignment: _____ Level: _____

	Level 1	Level 2	Level 3	Level 4
Understanding Concepts	Demonstrates a limited understanding of the concepts. Requires teacher intervention.	Demonstrates a basic understanding of the concepts.	Demonstrates a good understanding of the concepts.	Demonstrates a thorough understanding of the concepts.
Response to the Text	Expresses responses to the text with limited effectiveness, inconsistently supported by proof from the text	Expresses responses to the text with some effectiveness, supported by some proof from the text	Expresses responses to the text with appropriate skills, supported with appropriate proof	Expresses thorough and complete responses to the text, supported by concise and effective proof from the text
Analysis & Application of Concepts	Interprets and applies various concepts in the text with few, unrelated details and incorrect analysis	Interprets and applies various concepts in the text with some detail, but with some inconsistent analysis	Interprets and applies various concepts in the text with appropriate detail and analysis	Effectively interprets and applies various concepts in the text with consistent, clear and effective detail and analysis

STRENGTHS:

WEAKNESSES:

NEXT STEPS:

Teacher Guide

Our resource has been created for ease of use by both *TEACHERS* and *STUDENTS* alike.

Introduction

This resource provides ready-to-use information and activities for remedial students in grades five to eight. Written to grade and using simplified language and vocabulary, social studies concepts are presented in a way that makes them more accessible to students and easier to understand. Comprised of reading passages, student activities and mini posters, our resource can be used effectively for whole-class, small group and independent work.

How Is Our Resource Organized?

STUDENT HANDOUTS

Reading passages and **activities** (*in the form of reproducible worksheets*) make up the majority of our resource. The reading passages present important grade-appropriate information and concepts related to the topic. Embedded in each passage are one or more questions that ensure students understand what they have read.

For each reading passage there are **BEFORE YOU READ** activities and **AFTER YOU READ** activities.

- The BEFORE YOU READ activities prepare students for reading by setting a purpose for reading. They stimulate background knowledge and experience, and guide students to make connections between what they know and what they will learn. Important concepts and vocabulary from the chapters are also presented.

- The AFTER YOU READ activities check students' comprehension of the concepts presented in the reading passage and extend their learning. Students are asked to give thoughtful consideration of the reading passage through creative and evaluative short-answer questions, research, and extension activities.

Writing Tasks are included to further develop students' thinking skills and understanding of the concepts. The **Assessment Rubric** (*page 4*) is a useful tool for evaluating students' responses to many of the activities in our resource. The **Comprehension Quiz** (*page 48*) can be used for either a follow-up review or assessment at the completion of the unit.

PICTURE CUES

This resource contains three main types of pages, each with a different purpose and use. A **Picture Cue** at the top of each page shows, at a glance, what the page is for.

Teacher Guide
- Information and tools for the teacher

Student Handout
- Reproducible worksheets and activities

Easy Marking™ Answer Key
- Answers for student activities

EASY MARKING™ ANSWER KEY

Marking students' worksheets is fast and easy with this **Answer Key**. Answers are listed in columns – just line up the column with its corresponding worksheet, as shown, and see how every question matches up with its answer!

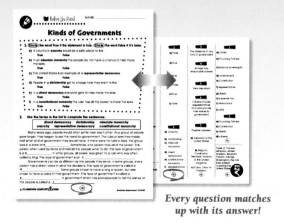

Every question matches up with its answer!

Bloom's Taxonomy

Our resource is an effective tool for any SOCIAL STUDIES PROGRAM.

Bloom's Taxonomy* for Reading Comprehension

The activities in our resource engage and build the full range of thinking skills that are essential for students' reading comprehension and understanding of important social studies concepts. Based on the six levels of thinking in Bloom's Taxonomy, and using language at a remedial level, information and questions are given that challenge students to not only recall what they have read, but move beyond this to understand the text and concepts through higher-order thinking. By using higher-order skills of application, analysis, synthesis and evaluation, students become active readers, drawing more meaning from the text, attaining a greater understanding of concepts, and applying and extending their learning in more sophisticated ways.

Our resource, therefore, is an effective tool for any Social Studies program. Whether it is used in whole or in part, or adapted to meet individual student needs, our resource provides teachers with essential information and questions to ask, inspiring students' interest, creativity, and promoting meaningful learning.

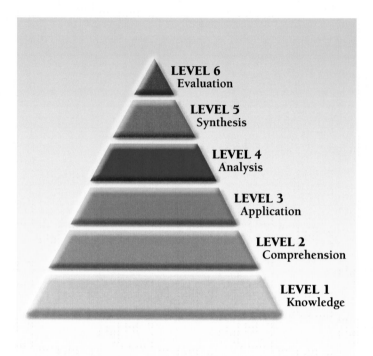

BLOOM'S TAXONOMY: 6 LEVELS OF THINKING

Bloom's Taxonomy is a widely used tool by educators for classifying learning objectives, and is based on the work of Benjamin Bloom.

Vocabulary

• authority • leader • necessary • rights • defend • common good • legislate • enforce • conflicts • security • dictatorship • anarchy • monarchy • absolute • representative • constitutional • democracy • liberty • constitution • amendment • supreme law • citizen • Founding Fathers • executive • legislative • judiciary • ratify • popular • sovereignty • Senate • Congress • House of Representatives • cabinet • president • vice-president • Supreme Court • separation • justices • veto • system • agencies • override • reprieve • pardon • impeach • resign • purpose • debate • sponsor • propose • clerk • hopper • committee • approve • majority • electors • candidate • requirement • political party • campaign • election • nominate • presides • consecutive • Democrat • Republican

NAME: _____

What Is Government?

1. **Use a straight line to match each word to its meaning. Use a dictionary to help.**

rights		able to control someone or something	**A**
leader		the person or people who make the rules or laws for everyone else	**B**
power		to create or pass laws	**C**
authority		to make or keep safe from danger, attack, or harm	**D**
legislate		one who is in charge or in command of others	**E**
enforce		something that is due to a person or government by law, tradition, or nature	**F**
defend		the power that someone has because of custom, law, or consent of those being governed	**G**
government		to command obedience to	**H**

2. **Complete each sentence with the correct term from the list. Use a dictionary to help.**

security	conflict	consent	common good	necessary

a) A system of government is _____ to keep order in society.

b) When two people or two countries disagree about something, they have a _____ about it.

c) A government that looks out for the well-being of all its citizens works for the _____ of everyone in the country.

d) Giving your approval is another way of saying that you give your _____.

e) A government should provide for the safety or _____ of its citizens.

What Is Government?

Each nation in the world has some form of government. The person or group of people who makes the rules or laws for everyone else is called a **government**. This person or group has the power or **authority** to do this. The **leader** or leaders of a government are the ones who take charge and make plans. Leaders can be chosen by the people or they can use force to take charge. There are many kinds of governments in the world.

> Governments are instituted among Men, deriving their just Powers from the Consent of the Governed....
>
> Thomas Jefferson, The Declaration of Independence, 1776

Why Do We Need Governments?

Imagine what life would be like if there were no rules. People could do or say anything they wanted. They could take your things or hurt you and no one would punish them. Now think what a country full of people would be like with no rules or laws. This isn't a pleasant thought, is it? A government is **necessary** to protect our **rights**.

A government should **defend** or keep its citizens safe. Doing this is called looking out for the **common good** of the people. Governments **legislate** or make and **enforce** laws to make sure all the people are treated fairly and with dignity. Sometimes two or more countries have **conflicts** or disagreements with each other that may even lead to a war.

STOP

Why do you think people need some kind of government? Give at least three reasons.

_____

_____

_____

What Is Government?

1. **Fill in each blank with the correct term from the list. Some terms will be left over.**

rights	leader	power	authority	legislate	enforce	necessary
defend	government	security	conflicts	consent	common good	

Suppose you want to start a brand new country. Your first step would be to make sure of the people's safety or _____. To do this, you would need to appoint
a
the person or group of people who would make the rules or laws for everyone else. This group is also called the _____.
b
Governments are _____ to keep order in society. They provide a system
c
of rules or laws to follow when people have disagreements or _____
d
with each other. The _____ of this country is the one who is in charge or in
e
command of all the others. This person in charge will have the _____ or
f
power to give orders to other members of the government. Everyone in the government should work for the _____ or well-being of all of the citizens.
g
Some of the citizens will _____, or keep from danger, the rest of the people.
h
Hopefully, this country of yours will be successful.

2. Why do you think it is **very important** to make sure that all of the citizens of a country are safe?

_____

3. If two countries have a conflict with each other, name **two** ways they can resolve or settle it.

_____

4. How are those who serve in the government selected in your country?

_____

Kinds of Governments

1. **Complete each sentence with a term from the list. Use a dictionary to help you.**

> dictatorship   anarchy   absolute monarchy   direct democracy
> constitutional monarchy   representative democracy

a) _____ exists when a nation has no government at all.

b) A(n) _____ is a form of government with a ruler who inherits the position, rules for life, and holds all power.

c) In a _____, the supreme power is held by all the people and is used by them directly.

d) In a _____, all power is held by one person who may use force.

e) In a _____, voters choose their government representatives.

f) In a _____, the power of the ruler or monarch is limited by law.

2. **Write down each kind of government in the correct box. Use the word list from Question 1 above.**

a) Total rule by one person, usually a king or queen _____	**b)** All citizens take part in suggesting and making laws _____	**c)** Voters choose representatives to act in their interests _____
d) Exists when a leader rules with absolute power, usually by force _____	**e)** Exists when a nation has no person or group in charge, and people can do anything they wish _____	**f)** Government lead by a monarch whose power is limited by law _____

Kinds of Governments

When we study the countries of the world we find that each one has some kind of government. The government of a country is the person or group of people who makes the rules or laws for everyone else. Governments can be set up in many different ways.

Governments set limits for the people. The first job of a government is to protect the people's rights. If there were no government, people could say and do anything they wished. This would be called **anarchy**.

The laws of a government tell how much power the ruler or leader has. These laws should also insure that all the people are treated in a fair and respectful manner.

What do you think? In an anarchy, people can do or say anything they wish to another person. Do you think this would be a good situation? Why or why not?

_____

There are about 200 different countries in the world. Not all of them have the same type of government. Here are some of the main kinds of governments:

GOVERNMENT	HOW IT WORKS
Absolute monarchy	- Total rule by one person who makes all the laws for all the people - Usually, the ruler is called a king or queen - Only a few nations in the world have absolute monarchies
Constitutional monarchy	- A form of government where the power of the ruler or monarch is limited by law - The government is usually made up of representatives elected by the people - There are many constitutional monarchies today
Dictatorship	- A country whose leader rules with absolute power, usually by force - Some dictatorships still exist today
Direct democracy	- A system of government in which all the citizens take part in suggesting and making the laws - The ancient city-state of Athens in Greece is a good example of a direct democracy
Representative democracy	- A system of government in which voters choose representatives to act in their interests - The United States is an example of a modern representative democracy
Anarchy	- Exists when there is no government present in a country - The people can do or say anything they wish to anyone

Kinds of Governments

1. **Circle** the word True if the statement is true. **Circle** the word False if it's false.

   a) A country in **anarchy** would be a safe place to live.

   True   **False**

   b) In an **absolute monarchy** the people do not have a chance to help make the laws.

   True   **False**

   c) The United States is an example of a **representative democracy**.

   True   **False**

   d) People in a **dictatorship** get to choose how they want to live.

   True   **False**

   e) In a **direct democracy** everyone gets to help make the laws.

   True   **False**

   f) In a **constitutional monarchy** the ruler has all the power to make the laws.

   True   **False**

2. Use the terms in the list to complete the sentences.

direct democracy	**dictatorship**	**absolute monarchy**
anarchy	**representative democracy**	**constitutional monarchy**

Many years ago, people would often settle near each other. As a group of people grew larger, they began to see the need for government. The rules or laws they made told what kind of government they would have. If there were no rules or laws, the group was in a state of _____**a**_____. Sometimes, one person took all of the power. This person often ruled by force and told all the people what to do. This type of government is a _____**b**_____. In other groups, all power was given to a ruler who was often called a king. This type of government is an _____**c**_____.

Governments can be as different as the people they serve. In some groups, every person has a direct voice in all of the decisions. This type of government is called a **d**_____. Some groups chose to have a king or queen, but also chose to have a voice in their government. This type of government is called a **e**_____. A government which has spokespeople to tell the wishes of the people is called a **f**_____.

Kinds of Governments

Answer each question with a complete sentence.

3. Describe **anarchy**.

_____

4. Which do you think would be a better kind of government – an **absolute monarchy** or a **constitutional monarchy**? Explain your decision.

_____

5. If you were designing a government, how important do you think the **rights** of each person should be?

_____

6. Write a brief description of a **representative democracy**.

_____

_____

7. Become a Research Detective!
Use an encyclopedia or the Internet to help you find the following:

a) Name one country whose government is a **representative democracy**.

_____

b) List the name of one country that is a **constitutional monarchy**.

_____

c) A few countries are still **dictatorships**. Find the name of one of them.

_____

NAME: _____

The Constitution of the U.S.A.

1. **Complete each sentence with a term from the list. Use a dictionary to help you.**

| Constitution | liberty | democracy | supreme law | citizen | amendment |
| popular sovereignty | | representative | ratify | Founding Fathers | |

a) A person who has rights within a government is called a _____.

b) The signers of the U.S. Declaration of Independence or the U.S. Constitution are called the _____.

c) _____ is the belief that the people of a country should hold supreme power.

d) A change in a law is called an _____.

e) A set of written rules which set up a government are called the _____.

f) A person who is chosen to state the beliefs of and to make laws for others is called a _____.

g) Another word for freedom is _____.

h) The highest or most powerful law in the country is called the _____.

i) A _____ is a form of government in which the people choose who governs them.

j) _____ also means to approve something.

2. **Use the terms in the list above to fill in each blank.**

See the signatures of the _____ _____!
a

A copy of the _____ of the
b

United States of America and the Declaration of Independence

will be on display tomorrow in the library!

Examine the names of all the men who signed them.

Learn about the fight for _____ and justice!
c

Imagine that you are one of the first _____ of the U.S.A.!
d

The Constitution of the U.S.A.

A Little History

The King of England ruled the American colonies for years. Finally, in 1776, a group of American men wanted to tell the king just how much the Americans wanted to be free of English rule. They chose Thomas Jefferson to write The **Declaration of Independence**. The Declaration told the king that the Americans believed that all men were created equal. They also believed that all men had certain rights including the right to life, liberty, and the pursuit of happiness.

Of course, King George was very angry. He sent British troops to America to control the colonists. This was the beginning of the **Revolutionary War**, also known as the **War for Independence**. The war went on for seven long years. **George Washington** was the **Commander-in-Chief** of the American forces in the fight for **liberty**. Then, in 1783, the Americans won the war.

When the war ended, the next job was to write a plan for government and law for the new **United States of America**. Many men, including Thomas Jefferson, James Madison, Benjamin Franklin, and George Washington helped write the Constitution. These men, along with others, are called the **Founding Fathers** because of the role they played in starting the United States.

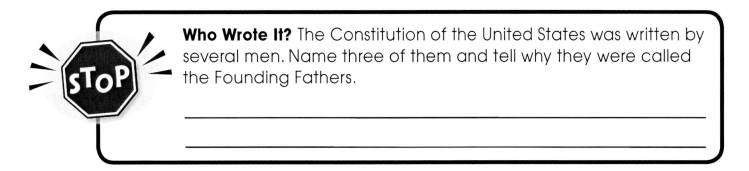

Who Wrote It? The Constitution of the United States was written by several men. Name three of them and tell why they were called the Founding Fathers.

_____

_____

What Is the Constitution?

The Constitution is the **supreme law** of the United States. It divides the government into three parts: **the executive, the legislative, and the judiciary**. It also states that any **citizen** may take part in the government by voting. Each of the states had to **ratify** or approve the Constitution.

The Constitution of the U.S.A.

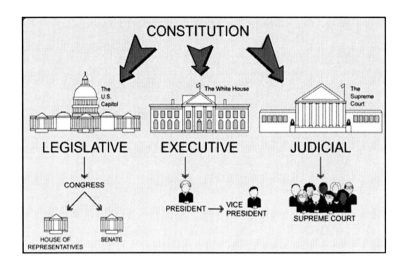

The government of the United States is based on the Constitution. It is set up as a **democracy** or a government in which the people choose who governs them. The belief that the people hold the highest power in a government is called **popular sovereignty**.

The U.S. Constitution can be added to or changed by **amendments**. In order for an amendment to become a law, the voters must approve it. The first ten amendments of the Constitution are called the **Bill of Rights**.

Each of the three parts of government has an important purpose. The Constitution describes each part and its purpose:

1. The purpose of the **legislative branch** of the government is to make laws. Voters throughout the United States choose people to represent them in either the **House of Representatives** or the **Senate**. These two groups combine to make up **Congress**.

2. The purpose of the **executive branch** is to make sure that the laws are obeyed. The executive branch is made up of the **president and vice-president** with help from the **cabinet** members or department heads.

3. Finally, the **judicial branch** of the government is composed of the members of the **Supreme Court** and all the lower federal courts in the land. The job of the judicial branch of government is to decide arguments about the meaning of laws, how they are applied, and whether they break the rules of the Constitution.

The Constitution of the U.S.A.

1. **Number the events from ❶ to ❺ in the order they happened.**

_____ **a)** King George sent troops to America.

_____ **b)** Thomas Jefferson wrote the Declaration of Independence.

_____ **c)** The Constitution of the United States was written and ratified.

_____ **d)** The War for Independence from Britain ended.

_____ **e)** George Washington served as Commander-in-Chief of the American forces.

2. Circle the word True if the statement is true. Circle the word False if it's false.

a) Benjamin Franklin wrote the Declaration of Independence.

True   **False**

b) Another name for the War for Independence is the Revolutionary War.

True   **False**

c) America won the War for Independence in 1780.

True   **False**

d) The U.S. Constitution is the basis for all other laws in the United States.

True   **False**

e) The Constitution divides the government into two parts.

True   **False**

NAME: _____

The Constitution of the U.S.A.

Answer each question with a complete sentence.

3. The Declaration of Independence stated that all men are created equal and have three basic rights. What are these **three basic rights**?

_____

_____

4. The Constitution divides the government into three branches. Each branch has a different purpose. What are the **three branches**?

_____

_____

5. Who chooses the representatives who will make the laws in a democracy?

_____

6. What is the **Bill of Rights**?

_____

_____

7. What does each branch of the U.S. government do?

_____

_____

8. Become a Research Detective!
Use an encyclopedia or the Internet to help you find the following:

You have learned about the Bill of Rights. In complete sentences tell the **main idea** of each of the Amendments (there are **ten**!). Write your answers on the chart on the next page.

Amendments to the Bill of Rights

Amendment 1	➡	**Main Idea**
Amendment 2	➡	**Main Idea**
Amendment 3	➡	**Main Idea**
Amendment 4	➡	**Main Idea**
Amendment 5	➡	**Main Idea**
Amendment 6	➡	**Main Idea**
Amendment 7	➡	**Main Idea**
Amendment 8	➡	**Main Idea**
Amendment 9	➡	**Main Idea**
Amendment 10	➡	**Main Idea**

NAME: _____

Three Branches of the Federal Government

Fill in each blank with the correct term. You may use a dictionary if you wish. Some terms will be used more than once. Some terms will be left over.

separation	powers	justices	judicial	legislative
Congress	The Senate	judiciary	The House of Representatives	
	executive	President	veto	bill

1. The three branches of the federal government are the _____ branch, the_____ branch, and the _____ branch.

2. The House of Representatives and the Senate are the divisions of _____.

3. Only the President can _____ or stop a bill from becoming a law.

4. The chief executive of the United States is called the _____.

5. Another name for Supreme Court judges is Supreme Court _____.

6. The branch of government which makes decisions about the laws of the land is called the _____ branch.

7. The branch of government which makes sure that the laws are followed is called the _____ branch.

8. The branch of government which enacts laws is called the _____ branch.

9. _____ of _____ means that one person or branch of government never has all power over the citizens.

10. Another name for a law that has not yet been approved by the President is a _____.

NAME: _____

Three Branches of the Federal Government

After the war with Britain, the writers of the Constitution knew that the best system of government would be one that split its control among two or more people or groups. This idea is called **separation of powers**. They gave the new government three branches. Each one would have its own jobs and responsibilities. Also, each branch would be able to check on the others' work. This is called a **system of checks and balances**. The goal would be to make sure that the citizens' rights were always protected.

The three branches of the U.S. government are the **legislative**, **executive**, and **judicial**. The Constitution describes the duties that each branch has and the titles of the people who carry out these duties. Each branch must follow the Constitution at all times. The headquarters for each branch of government is in Washington, D.C., the nation's capital.

The **executive branch** makes sure that the laws of the country are obeyed. The **President** is the head of the executive branch. The executive branch is very large because many people and groups are needed to help the President. The **Vice President** is the President's main helper. Others who assist are the President's **Cabinet**. Article Two of the Constitution established the executive branch.

STOP

Do You Know? What are the three branches of the United States government? Which document describes the duties of each branch?

_____

_____

The **judicial branch** answers questions about the meaning of laws and whether or not they follow the Constitution. The highest court in the judicial branch is called the **Supreme Court**. Nine judges or **Supreme Court Justices** make decisions about laws and other court matters. The head of the Supreme Court is called the **Chief Justice**. Article Three of the Constitution established the judicial branch.

Three Branches of the Federal Government

The **legislative branch** makes laws for the nation. It is made up of **Congress** and some **government agencies**. Article One of the Constitution established the legislative branch. Congress has two parts – the **House of Representatives** and the **Senate**.

Making a new law can take time. When members of Congress decide that there is a need for a new or different law one or more of them will **(1)** introduce their ideas to their house of Congress. At that time **the bill**, or proposed law, **(2)** will be studied by a committee. If the committee members believe that the country really does need the new law, they will vote "yes" and **(3)** send it to the other part of Congress. The other house members **(4)** will vote on the bill at that time. If they vote "yes", **(5)** the bill is then sent to the President of the United States. The President will study the bill and decide whether or not it should be a law. **(6)** If he signs the bill, it becomes a law. If he doesn't sign the bill it will not become a law. We can say that the President **vetoed** the bill. **(7)** A vetoed bill will be sent back to Congress for another vote. If two-thirds of the members of Congress approve the bill, it will become a law anyway. This process may take as long as two years to complete.

The writers of the Constitution worked very hard to make sure that the wishes and ideas of the citizens of the United States were included at every level of the government. This is truly what a **democratic** government is all about.

Look It Up! How many presidents has the United States had? Have any of them been father and son?

_____

_____

_____

NAME: _____

Three Branches of the Federal Government

1. **Circle** the word True if the statement is true. **Circle** the word False if it's false. If it is false, rewrite the statement to make it correct.

a) After the war with Britain, the writers of the Constitution wanted to have a monarchy.

True   **False**   _____

b) A system of checks and balances means that only Congress members can measure roads and check railroad train cars.

True   **False**   _____

c) The main goal of the separation of powers is to make sure that no person or group has all the power in the government.

True   **False**   _____

d) The main job of the executive branch of the government is to make sure that all laws are obeyed.

True   **False**   _____

e) The President's main helper is the Chief Justice of the Supreme Court.

True   **False**   _____

f) The judicial branch must make sure that all laws agree with the Constitution.

True   **False**   _____

g) The head of the Supreme Court is called the superior judge.

True   **False**   _____

h) The House of Representatives and the Senate make the laws for the country.

True   **False**   _____

i) It is not important for citizens' rights to be considered in government.

True   **False**   _____

Three Branches of the Federal Government

Answer the following questions in your notebook.

2. Compare the duties of the executive branch of government with those of the judicial branch.

3. Name three qualities that a good President of the United States should have.

4. The members of Congress represent all the people who live in their state or district. Why is it important for them to know how these people feel about the issues and problems that exist there?

5. **Become a Research Detective!**

Use an encyclopedia or the Internet to help you find the following:

The president's cabinet is made up of fifteen departments, several advisors and the Vice President.

The fifteen departments are listed below. What is the **main job** of each department? Write your answers in your notebook.

1. Department of State
2. Department of the Treasury
3. Department of Defense
4. Department of the Interior
5. Department of Justice
6. Department of Agriculture
7. Department of Commerce
8. Department of Labor
9. Department of Housing and Urban Development
10. Department of Transportation
11. Department of Energy
12. Department of Education Services
13. Department of Health and Human
14. Department of Veterans' Affairs
15. Department of Homeland Security

System of Checks and Balances

1. Write each term beside the correct meaning.

| override reprieve veto   pardon impeach resign constitutional democracy |
| checks and balances   executive branch   legislative branch   judicial branch |

- [ ] **a)** To forgive the actions or crimes of another

- [ ] **b)** A plan in which one branch of a government can make sure that other branches do not have too much power

- [ ] **c)** The president, vice president, and cabinet members

- [ ] **d)** A system of government in which the people choose who runs it

- [ ] **e)** To prevent from happening

- [ ] **f)** The House of Representatives and the Senate

- [ ] **g)** To stop or end a law

- [ ] **h)** To quit or leave office

- [ ] **i)** To bring a public official who is accused of wrong-doing before a group for judgment

- [ ] **j)** To end or take away a court sentence

- [ ] **k)** The federal court system and the U.S. Supreme Court

- [ ] **l)** Agreeing with the Constitution

2. Use a straight line to match each branch of U.S. government with the Article of the Constitution which established it.

1	Executive Branch		Article One	A
2	Judicial Branch		Article Two	B
3	Legislative Branch		Article Three	C

System of Checks and Balances

The government of the United States is built on a foundation of freedom. The writers of the Constitution knew that no single person or branch of government should ever have enough power to take away the freedom of the others. This is why they included a **system of checks and balances** in the Constitution. Each branch **checks**, or holds back, the other two. This helps to keep the balance of power even in all three branches.

The Checking Power of the Executive Branch

As the head of the executive branch, the President can check the power of the legislative branch by using his right to **veto**, or prevent, a bill from becoming a law. Each law approved by Congress is sent to the President for his approval. If he chooses not to approve the law, we say that it has been vetoed.

In fact, the President can approve or veto any law except one that amends, or changes, the Constitution. Having this ability gives the President strong checking power over the legislative branch. A two-thirds majority vote of the Congress is the only way to **override**, or stop, a presidential veto.

STOP

Food for Thought: How does a system of checks and balances protect freedom? Why is this important?

_____

_____

_____

The President can also check the power of the judicial branch of government in the following ways:

1. The president approves all federal judges and Supreme Court justices.

2. The president can **pardon**, or forgive, a person convicted of a federal crime.

3. The president can **reprieve**, or take away the punishment, of people who have been convicted of federal crimes.

System of Checks and Balances

The Checking Power of the Legislative Branch

Congress was also given strong checking abilities by the writers of the Constitution. Congress can check the executive branch by:

1. Overriding a president's veto

2. Approving treaties signed by the president

3. Impeaching, or placing on trial, any federal official including the president

4. Approving people appointed by the president for federal jobs

5. Cutting funding to federal departments

Congress can check the powers of the judicial branch by amending the Constitution.

The Checking Power of the Judicial Branch

The judicial branch can check the powers of both the executive and legislative branches. The writers of the Constitution made sure that these checks were in place in order to keep the balance of justice equal. The judicial branch checks the executive branch by deciding whether an action taken by the President or other member of the executive branch is **constitutional**, or agrees with the Constitution. Likewise, the judicial branch checks the legislative branch by judging whether a law passed by Congress is constitutional.

We can now see that a system of checks and balances is provided by the Constitution to make sure that every branch stays legal and constitutional. The insight shown by the writers of the Constitution in this area is one of the main reasons that the democratic government of the United States has prospered through the years.

System of Checks and Balances

1. **Use the words in the list to answer each question.**

checks	veto	override	pardon	reprieve	impeach	constitutional

[ ] **a)** What is the term for, "refusing to approve a bill or law"?

[ ] **b)** Which term means, "to place on trial"?

[ ] **c)** Which term means, "agrees with the Constitution"?

[ ] **d)** This term means, "to hold back or keep equal".

[ ] **e)** Which term means, "to stop a veto"?

[ ] **f)** This term means, "to forgive".

[ ] **g)** Which term means, "to take away the punishment"?

2. Circle the word True if the statement is true. Circle the word False if it's false.

a) Each branch of the U.S. government checks the other two.

  True   **False**

b) Presidents cannot be impeached.

  True   **False**

c) The President must approve all federal judges and justices of the Supreme Court.

  True   **False**

d) The judicial branch can decide whether or not a president's actions are constitutional.

  True   **False**

e) There are seven justices on the Supreme Court.

  True   **False**

NAME: _____

System of Checks and Balances

Answer each question with a complete sentence.

3. What is the **purpose** of a system of checks and balances in the U.S. government?

_____

_____

4. When might a president **pardon** someone who has been convicted of a federal crime?

_____

_____

5. Explain this statement: **"Freedom is the foundation of democracy"**.

_____

_____

6. Why do you think the writers of the Constitution were so firm about making sure no branch had more power than the other two? (Hint – remember the situation with England.)

_____

_____

7. What is the only means of **overriding** a presidential veto?

_____

_____

8. How can the judicial branch check the legislative branch?

_____

_____

NAME: _____

Divisions of Each Branch of Government

Vice-President of the United States	**Executive Branch**
divisions **Judicial Branch**	**Legislative Branch**
Speaker of the House of Representatives	**three**
Cabinet **Chief Executive of the United States**	**Congress**

1.   Use the terms above to complete the sentences.

The government of the United States of America is divided into _____
                                                                                                    a

branches. Each branch has several sections or _____. The role of the
                                                                                        b

_____ is to make sure that all of the laws of the United States are obeyed.
         c

The president is also known as the _____. The people
                                                                            d

who lead the 15 federal agencies that assist the president are called the President's

_____.
         e

The role of the _____ is to write, debate, and pass new
                                          f

laws. This branch is made up of the House of Representatives and the Senate. Together,

these sections are known as _____. The person who leads the House of
                                                g

Representatives is called the _____. The
                                                          h

_____ also serves as the President of the Senate.
            i

The Supreme Court is part of the _____. Its main job is
                                                                j

to answer questions about the meaning of laws and whether or not they follow the

Constitution of the United States.

Divisions of Each Branch of Government

As you have already learned, there are three branches of the federal government: **executive, legislative, and judicial**. The Constitution of the United States describes the duties of each one. Each branch has many sections or divisions. The people in each division work hard to make sure all of the work is done.

> that government of the people, by the people, for the people, shall not perish from the earth
>
> Abraham Lincoln

The Executive Branch

The President of the United States is the **Chief Executive** of the country. The president is the **head of the executive branch of government**. The president and his assistants make up the **Executive Office of the President (EOP)**. They have many jobs to do. One is to **oversee the White House operations**. Another is to **direct the office of the vice-president. Managing other councils** or groups of people is also a job of the EOP.

The U.S. Constitution gives the president the powers to do many things. The president appoints federal officials and members of the Supreme Court. The president and other EOP members work out treaties. Also, the president is the Commander in Chief of the armed forces. The President's **Cabinet** (group of advisors) also helps with the many duties of the EOP.

What Do You Think? Could the president complete all the duties of the Executive Office of the President alone? Why or why not?

_____

_____

The Legislative Branch

The legislative branch of the federal government includes the **House of Representatives and the Senate**. Together, these houses are called **Congress**. The jobs of Congress are to **write, debate, and pass new laws**.

Divisions of Each Branch of Government

The Constitution of the United States gives Congress several jobs to do. Congress can: (1) tax citizens, (2) borrow money, (3) print money, (4) pay the country's debts, (5) set up federal courts, (6) declare war, (7) raise an army, (8) have post offices, and (9) manage the District of Columbia.

Each section of Congress has a leader who oversees the law-making process. **The Vice-President of the United States is the leader (president pro-tempore) of the Senate. The Speaker of the House of Representatives is the leader of the House.**

The Judicial Branch

The judicial branch of the government **answers questions about the meaning of laws and whether or not they follow the Constitution.** The highest court in the land is the **United States Supreme Court.** <u>No person or court can overrule the decisions of the U.S. Supreme Court.</u> The federal court system is made up of: (1) the Supreme Court of the United States, (2) the U.S. Court of Military Appeals, (3) twelve U.S. Courts of Appeals, (4) the U.S. Court of Appeals for the Federal Circuit, and (5) the lower courts.

Use Your Brain! Thomas Jefferson said that there should be ***"jealous care taken of the right of election by the people."*** Write a paragraph describing the things that a voter should consider before voting for a candidate for President of the United States or governor of his state. Write your answer in your notebook.

After You Read

Divisions of Each Branch of Government

1. Circle the word True if the statement is true. Circle the word False if it's false.

a) The President's Cabinet is in the Oval Office and holds his important papers.

   True   **False**

b) One of the President's jobs is to be in charge of the Army, Navy, Marines, and Air Force.

   True   **False**

c) The Supreme Court has the power to tax people.

   True   **False**

d) The Military Court of Appeals can overturn the decisions of the United States Supreme Court.

   True   **False**

e) There are twelve U.S. Courts of Appeals.

   True   **False**

2. **Use the terms in the list to answer each question. Each term may be used more than once.**

| Executive Branch | Legislative Branch | Judicial Branch | President | Vice-President |

a) The President of the United States is the head of this branch of government.

b) This branch of government writes, debates, and passes new laws.

c) This branch of government oversees all military trials and legal business.

d) This branch of government has the authority to print money and declare war.

e) This person is the president pro-tempore of the Senate.

f) This person is the leader of the Executive Office of the President.

g) This branch of government answers questions about the U.S. Constitution.

h) This leader appoints Supreme Court justices.

Divisions of Each Branch of Government

Answer each question with a complete sentence.

3. Explain why a senator or congressman should have a good understanding of business and how to use money.

_____

4. In which branch of government would being an **attorney** (lawyer) be the greatest help? Why?

_____

5. Explain why the President of the United States needs to have a great ability to understand people and to encourage them to get along with each other.

_____

6. In your opinion, should the President of the United States stay at home in the White House all of the time or should he travel throughout the country and to other countries in the world? Why?

_____

_____

7. What does each branch of the federal government do? Complete the organizer on the next page.

8. **Become a Research Detective!**

Use your encyclopedia or Internet search engine to find the answer to the following:

Can a woman be President of the United States? If you find that women can be President, has there ever been one? When is the next presidential election in the United States?

_____

_____

NAME: _____

Divisions of Each Branch of Government

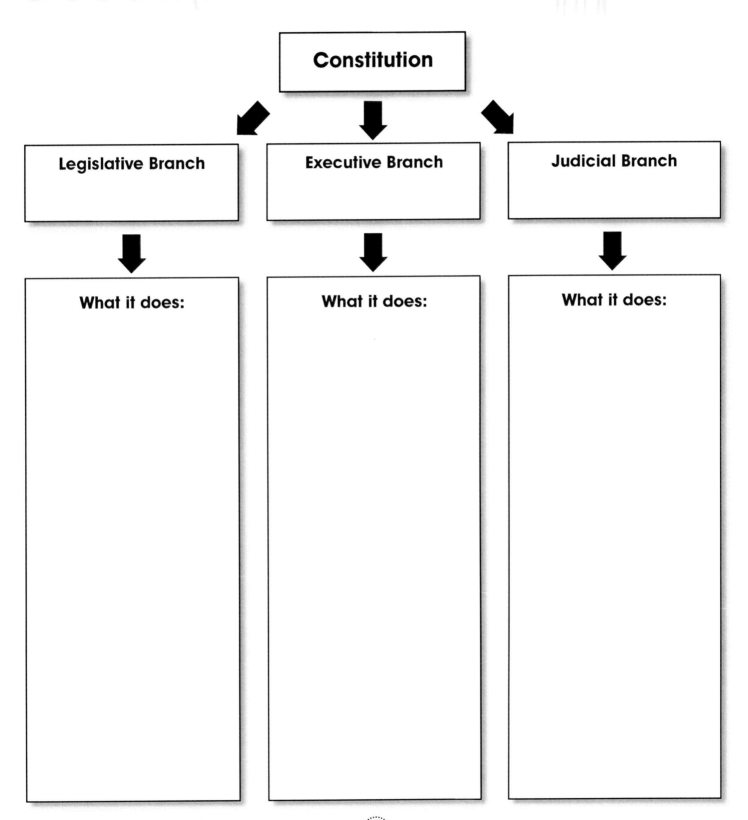

Constitution

Legislative Branch

Executive Branch

Judicial Branch

What it does:

What it does:

What it does:

NAME: _____

How a Bill Becomes a Law

1. **Write the correct word in each blank. Use the information in each sentence or a dictionary to help you. One word will be left over.**

sponsor	propose	table	bill	clerk	hopper	calendar
debate	committee	veto	override	approved		

a) A _____ is a suggestion for a law.

b) The person who introduces the bill to Congress is called its _____.

c) All suggestions for laws are handed to the _____ or put in the _____ on his desk.

d) After they are introduced, all bills go to a _____, or smaller group of legislators to be studied and discussed.

e) The committee then decides to release the bill or to _____ or lay it aside.

f) If the bill is released, it is placed on a list of bills awaiting action on a _____.

g) The bill then goes to the entire House of Representatives or Senate for discussion and _____.

h) A bill is _____ and sent to the president after both houses of Congress have passed it.

i) If the president decides that the bill is unneeded or unwise he can _____ it.

j) Congress can _____ the president's veto with a two-thirds majority vote.

2. **Use a straight line to match each word to its definition.**

sponsor	to suggest	**A**
veto	discussion	**B**
propose	a draft of a proposed law	**C**
debate	one who proposes a law	**D**
bill	to say no, or forbid the passage of a law	**E**

How a Bill Becomes a Law

Have you ever thought that there should be a law for or against something? If so, you have taken the first step on the path to a bill becoming one of the laws of the land. Every law made by Congress starts with someone's idea. Of course, only a member of Congress can suggest or **propose** it.

1. Think About It!   Suppose you have a good idea for a new law. Could YOU, PERSONALLY, suggest the law in Congress? Why or why not? Who are the only people who can propose a new law to the Senate of the House of Representatives?

_____

The legislator who proposes the bill is its **sponsor**. A bill's sponsor places the bill in a special box on the Speaker of the House of Representatives' desk called a **hopper**. The bill is then given a name and number which means it is ready for its **"first reading"**. The first reading of a bill means the bill's title is read on the House Floor. The bill is then sent to a **committee** or smaller group of legislators.

When a bill is in committee, the lawmakers study and **debate** or discuss it. Then, if they feel that the country needs this new law, they will vote to send the bill back to the House or Senate. When this happens the entire House or Senate votes on the bill. If it is approved, the bill is sent to the other part of Congress and the process begins again.

Finally, if the bill is approved by both houses of Congress, it is sent to the President for his approval. The President can either approve the bill, refuse to approve, or **veto**. When a presidential veto occurs, the bill goes back to Congress for another vote. If it is approved by a **two-thirds or more majority**, it becomes a law anyway. If it is not approved, the process is over.

2. See What's Happening in Congress!   Go to http://clerk.house. gov/floorsummary/floor.html and pull up today's date. You will get a summary of all the bills being considered. In your notebook, write down the number and a summary of one of the bills.

How a Bill Becomes a Law

1.   Fill in each blank with a term from the list.

sponsor	propose	table	bill	clerk	hopper	yes	no
debate	committee	veto	override	first reading		two-thirds majority	

Anyone can have an idea for a new law or _____, but a member of

a

Congress has to _____ it. The member of Congress who introduces the bill is

b

called its _____. He or she will place the written text of the bill on the desk

c

of the person in charge or in a special box called a _____. The bill is given a

d

name and is ready to be introduced to the group. This introduction is called the bill's

_____ _____. From there, the bill goes to a smaller group of people

e

called a _____ for discussion and _____. If this group decides

f   g

that the bill should not be a law, they put it aside or _____ it. If this group

h

of people decides that the bill should become a law they send it back to the entire

group in the House of Representatives or the Senate. There it is discussed and voted on.

If a majority of the members vote _____, the bill goes to the other part of

i

Congress and undergoes the same process again. If the bill is approved by both sections

of Congress, it is sent to the president of the United States. He can either approve the

bill or say no or _____ it. If the president says no to the bill it can go back

j

to Congress for another vote. If the bill wins a _____ _____,

k

Congress can _____ the president's veto and the bill becomes a law

l

anyway. If it does not, the process ends.

2.   Become a Research Detective!
Use the Internet to find out the sponsor(s) of one bill that is being considered in
Congress now. Write a complete sentence telling the number of the bill and who the
sponsor(s) is. Write your answer in your notebook.

How a Bill Becomes a Law

3. **Number the events from ❶ to ❾ in the order they occur.**

_____ **a)** The president approves the bill or does not approve or vetoes it.

_____ **b)** The bill goes to a smaller group called a committee for discussion and debate.

_____ **c)** A bill is introduced by a member of Congress who sponsors it.

_____ **d)** The entire group votes on the bill.

_____ **e)** The bill is named and read to the entire group which is its "first reading".

_____ **f)** If the entire group approves the bill, it goes to the other part of Congress.

_____ **g)** The committee approves the bill and returns it to the group for a vote.

_____ **h)** Both sections of Congress approve the bill and send it to the President.

_____ **i)** The bill goes back to Congress for another vote. If it gets a two-thirds majority approval, it becomes a law anyway. If not, the process is ended.

Answer each question with a complete sentence.

4. Why do you think the law-making process has so many different parts? (Hint – remember that this is a democracy where people's opinions matter greatly.)

_____

5. Does the president have more power in the law-making process than the Congress? Why or why not?

_____

6. Do you think that the law-making process is a very quick one? Why or why not?

_____

7. How can the voters have a part in the legislative process?

_____

Electing a Government

Write the correct term in each blank. You may use your dictionary if you wish.

electors   candidate   requirements to run for the presidency   presides
eight   requirements to run for the vice-presidency   the Vice-President
political party   primary elections   nominate   presidential term
campaign   major political parties in the U.S.   Senate term   election
House of Representatives term   state governments   consecutive

1. Democrats and Republicans

2. succeeds the president if he is not able to serve

3. the activities which are designed to help a person get elected to public office

4. to select or choose

5. a person who wants to hold public office

6. directs or runs

7. one after the other

8. six years

9. a group with the same ideas about running the government

10. four years

11. people who belong to the Electoral College

12. the time when citizens vote for the candidates of their choice

13. born in the U.S., at least 35 years old, and have lived in the U.S. for 14 years.

14. two years

15. generally are set up in the same manner as the federal government

Electing a Government

 Since the United States is a democracy, all of its government leaders are **elected**, or chosen by the citizens. The Constitution states all the requirements for each federal office. These must be fulfilled before a person can run for the office. A candidate for President or Vice-President of the United States must: **(1) be a citizen born in the United States, (2) be at least 35 years old, and (3) have lived in the United States for the last fourteen years. The office of the vice-president is also very important because the vice-president is the person who takes over as president if something happens that makes the president unable to serve.** The Constitution also sets the term limits for all federal offices. The President can only serve **two consecutive terms** (a total of eight years). The presidential elections are held every four years. Elections for the Senate are held every six years and those for the House of Representatives are held every two years. A person who runs for a political office is called a **candidate**.

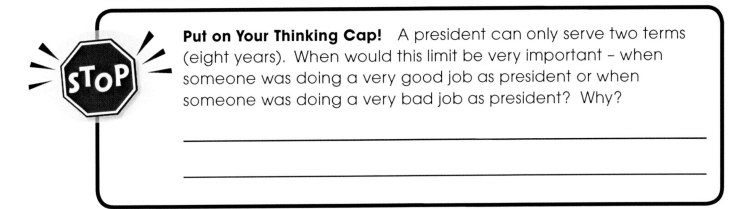

Put on Your Thinking Cap! A president can only serve two terms (eight years). When would this limit be very important – when someone was doing a very good job as president or when someone was doing a very bad job as president? Why?

_____

_____

Political Parties

In the United States there are two main political parties made up of groups of people who share the same ideas about how they think the government should be conducted. These parties are the **Democrats** and the **Republicans**.

Electing a Government

The president and vice-president are elected by a series of votes. The first vote is the direct or popular, vote in which registered voters go to the polls and vote for the candidate of their choice. The second vote is an indirect vote in which the **electors** chosen by the people vote for president and vice-president. The group of electors is called the Electoral College. The candidates for president and vice-president run together on the election ticket.

Candidates for other offices also appear on the ballot with the candidates for president. This enables citizens to vote for their choice for several offices at one time. Often, more than one person from a political party desires the same office. When this happens, **primary elections** are held in which the people vote for the candidate of their choice. The one who gets the most votes is the party's candidate in the election.

Other Offices

Since a presidential election only happens every four years, other offices are often the center of attention in other years. Citizens become very interested in their choices for senators and representatives. Since state governments are set up in the same way that the federal government is, folks are often voting for their choices for governor, lieutenant governor, and representatives to the state assemblies and senate. Local elections are carried out in a similar fashion.

Getting Elected

Being elected President of the United States is a very hard job. It takes lots of money and many supporters to mount a campaign for the presidency. Today, running for any office can be costly and time-consuming. People who want to serve in public office must be dedicated and prepared for hard work.

Be In the Know   Use a reference book or the Internet to do the following work. Make a chart of all the presidents of the United States. Begin with George Washington and end with the present President. Be sure to include the date the person was elected, the dates he or she held office, the name of the vice-president, and the political party of the president.

Electing a Government

1. **(Circle)** the word True if the statement is true. **(Circle)** the word False if it's false.

a) In a democracy only a few of the government leaders are elected by the citizens.

   True   **False**

b) A person who was born in Canada could become President of the United States.

   True   **False**

c) A presidential term lasts for four years.

   True   **False**

d) A person must be 40 years old to run for president of the United States.

   True   **False**

e) Primary elections are held when more than one person desires the same political office.

   True   **False**

f) It is not very difficult to run for the presidency of the United States.

   True   **False**

2. **Write each term beside its meaning.**

electors	candidate	campaign	major political parties in the U.S.
Vice-President	House of Representatives term		presidential term

[_____] **a)** Democrats and Republicans

[_____] **b)** Becomes president if the president cannot serve for some reason

[_____] **c)** Four years

[_____] **d)** A person who is running for public office

[_____] **e)** Two years

[_____] **f)** Activities which are designed to help a person get elected to public office.

[_____] **g)** People who belong to the Electoral College

NAME: _____

Electing a Government

Answer each question with a complete sentence.

3. Describe at **least three reasons** that could keep a person who would like to be president of the United States from running for that office. (Hint – remember the requirements stated in the Constitution and also what it takes to run a campaign for the presidency.)

_____

_____

4. Before 1951 presidents could serve for many terms. Franklin D. Roosevelt was elected four times! The **Twenty-second Amendment** limited a president's consecutive terms to two terms. Tell why you think this amendment was passed.

_____

_____

5. What do we call the chief executive of a state? Discuss some of the **jobs** that you think a state chief executive would have.

_____

_____

6. Describe the qualities you think that a person who wants to be the President of the United States should have.

_____

_____

7. Become a Research Detective!
Use your reference books or the Internet to find out how many Presidents of the United States have not completed their terms in office and why. List the name of the president, the reason for not completing the term, and the cause for not completing the term.

_____

_____

Here are six writing tasks about the government of the United States. Be sure to think about all that you have learned about the United States government as you write. Write your answers in complete sentences in your notebook.

Task #1   Every country on earth has some kind of government even though all governments are not alike. Organize your thoughts and knowledge about government and discuss the purpose(s) of government. In the United States' system of government, who or what are most important?

Task #2   The Constitution of the United States has a very important purpose for its government. What is that purpose? What is the Constitution sometimes called?

Task #3   The Declaration of Independence states that all citizens have certain rights. What are three of these rights? What document gives the citizens these and other rights?

Task #4   Rights always come along with responsibilities. Think about the rights you discussed in Writing Task 3 as well as others. Discuss at least one of the responsibilities that comes along with them.

Task #5   All countries have problems which must be solved. Some of these problems are so serious that they are present in most countries (for example, poverty). If you were president of the United States, which three problems would you try to solve? What would you do to solve them?

Task #6   The powers of all three branches of the U.S. government are equal. What document limits the powers of each branch? What is this limiting of powers called? Do you think that these limitations are good or bad? Tell why.

NAME: _____

Crossword Puzzle!

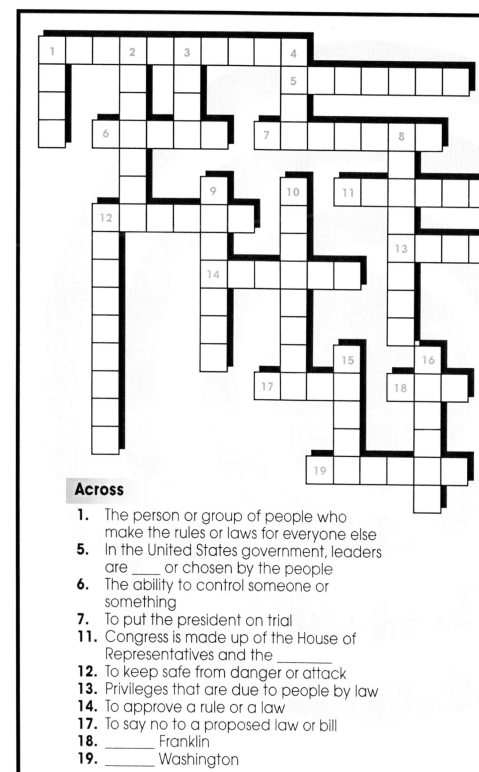

Word List

impeach	rights
enforce	nine
ratify	elected
Congress	nominate
government	Senate
House	resign
Ben	George
democracy	good
	power
	term
	defend
	anarchy
	veto

Across

1. The person or group of people who make the rules or laws for everyone else
5. In the United States government, leaders are ____ or chosen by the people
6. The ability to control someone or something
7. To put the president on trial
11. Congress is made up of the House of Representatives and the _____
12. To keep safe from danger or attack
13. Privileges that are due to people by law
14. To approve a rule or a law
17. To say no to a proposed law or bill
18. _____ Franklin
19. _____ Washington

Down

1. A government should provide for the common ____ of its citizens
2. To command obedience to
3. The number of justices (judges) on the U.S. Supreme Court
4. Length of time in elected office
8. Makes federal laws
9. Exists when there is no government in a country
10. To choose or select
12. A form of government in which the people choose who governs them
15. The ____ of Representatives
16. To quit or leave office

Word Search

Find all of the words in the Word Search. Words may be horizontal, vertical, or diagonal. A few may even be backwards! Look carefully!

government	powers	anarchy	resign
veto	branch	ratify	laws
congress	legislate	run	leader
vote	election	party	debate
checks	democracy	justice	war
senator	president	constitutional	clerk
bill	poll	judges	campaign

g	a	b	c	d	e	f	h	i	j	k	l	m	n	o	n	p	q
r	o	s	t	u	s	m	s	e	t	v	w	j	u	d	g	e	s
r	x	v	y	r	z	a	b	c	d	e	f	u	g	h	i	i	w
j	a	k	e	l	l	m	c	h	e	c	k	s	n	o	s	p	a
q	r	w	s	r	t	o	u	v	w	x	y	t	z	a	e	b	l
c	o	d	e	f	n	g	h	i	o	j	k	i	l	m	r	n	o
p	p	q	r	g	s	m	t	t	u	v	w	c	x	y	z	a	b
c	d	e	r	f	g	h	e	i	j	k	l	e	t	a	b	e	d
m	n	e	o	p	q	v	r	n	s	e	t	c	u	v	w	e	x
y	s	z	a	b	c	d	e	f	t	g	l	h	i	j	m	k	l
s	m	n	o	p	e	q	r	o	s	e	t	e	u	o	v	w	x
y	z	a	b	c	m	d	v	e	r	f	g	h	c	i	j	k	n
l	m	l	n	o	e	p	q	k	r	s	t	r	u	t	v	o	w
x	s	e	n	a	t	o	r	y	z	a	a	b	c	d	i	e	f
g	h	a	i	j	a	k	l	m	n	c	o	n	p	t	q	o	r
s	t	d	u	v	l	w	x	y	y	z	a	b	a	c	d	e	n
h	f	e	g	h	s	i	j	k	l	m	n	n	o	r	p	q	r
c	s	r	a	t	i	f	y	n	g	i	a	p	m	a	c	t	u
n	v	w	x	y	g	z	a	b	c	d	e	f	g	h	i	h	j
a	k	l	p	r	e	s	i	d	e	n	t	m	n	o	p	q	y
r	r	s	o	t	l	u	v	w	x	y	z	p	a	r	t	y	a
b	i	l	l	b	c	d	e	f	g	h	i	j	k	u	l	m	n
o	p	q	l	a	n	o	i	t	u	t	i	t	s	n	o	c	r

NAME: _____

Comprehension Quiz

Part A

/25

(Circle) the word True if the statement is true. (Circle) the word False if it's false.
If it is false, rewrite the statement to make it correct.

1. A government is the person or group who makes the rules for all the other citizens in a country.

True   **False**   _____

2. Governments are not necessary in all countries.

True   **False**   _____

3. Most governments in the Western Hemisphere are monarchies.

True   **False**   _____

4. The Declaration of Independence was written after the Revolutionary War in order to set up a government for the new country.

True   **False**   _____

5. Many men helped write the Constitution of the United States.

True   **False**   _____

6. The Supreme Law of the United States is the Declaration of Independence.

True   **False**   _____

7. In a country with popular sovereignty the citizens hold the highest power in the government.

True   **False**   _____

8. The only way to change the Constitution of the United States is by the vote of the Supreme Court.

True   **False**   _____

9. The Supreme Court is the only branch of government in which the people cannot directly vote for its members.

True   **False**   _____

10. The executive branch of government includes the vice-president and his staff.

True   **False**   _____

SUBTOTAL: **/10**

After You Read 📖

Comprehension Quiz

Part B

Answer each question in complete sentences.

1. Explain why the framers of the Constitution built a system of **checks and balances** into the three branches of government.

_____

_____

_____

2. Briefly tell how a bill becomes a federal law.

_____

_____

3. Describe the qualifications a person must have to run for **president** or **vice-president** of the United States.

_____

_____

4. Name each **branch** of the federal government and tell what each one does.

_____

_____

5. What form(s) of government is the best for its citizens and why?

_____

_____

_____

SUBTOTAL: /15

1.
a) citizen
b) Founding Fathers
c) popular sovereignty
d) amendment
e) Constitution
f) representative
g) liberty
h) supreme law
i) democracy
j) ratify

2.
a) Founding Fathers
b) Constitution
c) liberty
d) citizens
(14)

Three of: Thomas Jefferson, James Madison, Benjamin Franklin, George Washington; the role they played in starting the United States
(15)

3. The absence of any kind of government

4. Accept any reasonable answer

5. Very important

6. Citizens choose representatives to communicate their wishes to government

7. Possible answers:
a) Germany or the United States
b) Belgium, Cambodia, Denmark, Norway or the United Kingdom
c) Cuba, Libya or Pakistan
(13)

1.
a) False
b) True
c) True
d) False
e) True
f) False

2.
a) anarchy
b) dictatorship
c) absolute monarchy
d) direct democracy
e) constitutional monarchy
f) representative democracy
(12)

1.
a) Anarchy
b) absolute monarchy
c) direct democracy
d) dictatorship
e) representative democracy
f) constitutional monarchy

2.
a) absolute monarchy
b) direct democracy
c) representative democracy
d) dictatorship
e) anarchy
f) constitutional monarchy
(10)

Accept any reasonable answer
(11)

Possible answers: To settle disagreements; to protect citizens from other countries; to educate the citizens
(8)

1.
a) security
b) government
c) necessary
d) conflicts
e) leader
f) authority
g) common good
h) defend

2. Accept any reasonable answer

3. Accept any reasonable answer

4. Accept any reasonable answer
(9)

1.
A power
B government
C legislate
D defend
E leader
F rights
G authority
H enforce

2.
a) necessary
b) conflict
c) common good
d) consent
e) security
(7)

1.
a) pardon
b) checks and balances
c) executive branch
d) democracy
e) override
f) legislative branch
g) veto
h) resign
i) impeach
j) reprieve
k) judicial branch
l) constitutional

2.
1 B
2 C
3 A
(25)

Accept any reasonable answer
(26)

---

2. Accept any reasonable answer

3. Accept any reasonable answer

4. Accept any reasonable answer

5.

1 work with other countries to carry out president's foreign policy
2 set financial policy, set tax policy, print currency
3 direct and control U.S. armed forces
4 manage federal lands and natural resources
5 make sure federal laws are obeyed, supervise federal prisons, act as top lawyer for the U.S., give legal advice to president and other cabinet members
6 find ways to improve farming, inspect food
7 set up trade agreements with other countries, help American businesses that trade with other countries, explore oceans, give weather information, take census, grant patents
8 make rules for worker safety, help unemployed people, enforce federal labor laws
9 help people find homes, fund housing needs, provide loans for housing
10 direct transportation including the U.S. Coast Guard
11 advise president on the country's energy needs, study new energy sources
12 provide programs to improve education, enforce civil education laws, provide financial aid programs for students and parents, provide money for drug education
13 direct job programs for people with disabilities, help elderly and poor with financial needs, ensure the best health care for all citizens
14 provide benefits for veterans (i.e. pensions, medical services, survivors' benefits, Training)
15 evaluate threats from foreign terrorists, enforce homeland security laws, prevent further terrorist attacks
(24)

1.
a) False
b) False
c) True
d) False
e) True
f) True
g) False
h) True
i) False
(23)

---

1. legislative, executive, judiciary
2. Congress
3. veto
4. President
5. justices
6. judicial
7. executive
8. legislative
9. Separation, powers
10. bill
(20)

Legislative, executive, judicial; Constitution
(21)

In 2007, there have been 43 presidents. Two sets have been fathers and sons: John Adams & John Q. Adams, George H. Bush & George W. Bush
(22)

---

3. Life, liberty, and the pursuit of happiness

4. Executive, legislative, and judiciary

5. The citizens

6. The first 10 amendments of the Constitution of the U.S.

7. Executive – enforce the laws
Legislative – the laws
Judicial – make sure the laws are Constitutional

8.
1 – freedom of religion
2 – right to bear arms
3 – no soldiers quartered in private homes
4 – freedom from unreasonable search and seizure
5 – due process
6 – right to a speedy trial
7 – right to trial by jury
8 – no excessive bail
9 – guarantee of all rights
10 – powers not held by federal government belong to state governments
(18)

1.
a) 2
b) 1
c) 5
d) 4
e) 3

2.
a) False
b) True
c) False
d) True
e) False
(17)

EZ✓

1.
a) bill
b) sponsor
c) clerk, hopper
d) committee
e) table
f) calendar
g) debate
h) approved
i) veto
j) override

2.
A sponsor
B veto
C purpose
D debate
E bill

(36)

3. Accept any reasonable answer

4. Accept any reasonable answer

5. Accept any reasonable answer

6. Accept any reasonable answer

7. Legislative: makes laws for the nation
Executive: makes sure laws are obeyed
Judicial: answers questions about the meaning of laws, decides whether laws follow the constitution

8. Yes, a woman can be President. As of 2006, no woman has been president. The next election for president should be verified.

(34)

1.
a) False
b) True
c) False
d) False
e) True

2.
a) Executive
b) Legislative
c) Judicial
d) Legislative
e) Vice-President
f) President
g) Judicial
h) President

(33)

1.
a) three
b) divisions
c) Executive Branch
d) Chief Executive of the U.S.
e) Cabinet
f) Legislative Branch
g) Congress
h) Speaker of the House of Rep.
i) Vice-President of the U.S.
j) Judicial Branch

(30)

Accept any reasonable answer

(31)

Accept any reasonable answer

(32)

4. To keep the balance of power equal

5. Accept any reasonable answer

6. Accept any reasonable answer

7. Accept any reasonable answer

8. A two-thirds vote of Congress

9. Accept any reasonable answer

(29)

1.
a) veto
b) impeach
c) constitutional
d) check
e) override
f) pardon
g) reprieve

2.
a) True
b) False
c) True
d) True
e) False

(28)

Across:

1. government
5. elected
6. power
7. impeach
11. Senate
12. defend
13. rights
14. ratify
17. veto
18. Ben
19. George

Down:

1. good
2. enforce
3. nine
4. term
8. Congress
9. anarchy
10. nominate
12. democracy
15. House
16. resign

3.

age, place of birth, resources, etc.

4.

to restrict power

5.

governor

6.

Because the Vice President has to take over for the President if he is unable to serve

7.

Accept verified answers

Answers will vary

1.

a) False
b) False
c) True
d) False
e) True
f) False

2.

a) major political parties in the U.S.
b) Vice-President
c) presidential term
d) candidate
e) House of Rep. term
f) campaign
g) electors

1. major U.S. political parties
2. Vice-President
3. campaign
4. nominate
5. candidate
6. presides
7. consecutive
8. Senate term
9. political party
10. Presidential term
11. electors
12. election
13. President and Vice-President
14. House of Rep. term
15. state government

Accept any reasonable answer

Accept any answers that can be verified

3.

a) 8
b) 3
c) 1
d) 5
e) 2
f) 6
g) 4
h) 7
i) 9

4.

Accept any reasonable answer

5.

Accept any reasonable answer

6.

Accept any reasonable answer

7.

Accept any reasonable answer

1. No, only a member of congress can propose a law
2. Accept any answer that can be verified

1.

a) bill
b) propose
c) sponsor
d) hopper
e) first reading
f) committee
g) debate
h) table
i) yes
j) veto
k) two-thirds
l) override

2.

Accept any verifiable answer

Word Search Answers

Part A

1. True

2. False – governments are necessary

3. False – most are democracies

4. False

5. True

6. False – the Supreme Law is the Constitution

7. True

8. False – by the vote of citizens

9. True

10. True

Part B

1. Checks and balances help to make sure that one branch does not become more powerful than the other two

2. Bill is introduced in Congress. A committee decides what to do. Bill is discussed and voted on. Bill is approved by both houses of Congress. President acts on the bill. Bill becomes a law or is returned to Congress if the President vetoes it.

3. Same for both: citizen born in U.S., at least 35 years old, have lived in U.S. for the last 14 years

4. Executive: makes sure laws are obeyed
Legislative: makes laws for the nation
Judicial: answers questions about the meaning of laws, decides whether laws follow the constitution

5. Accept any reasonable answer

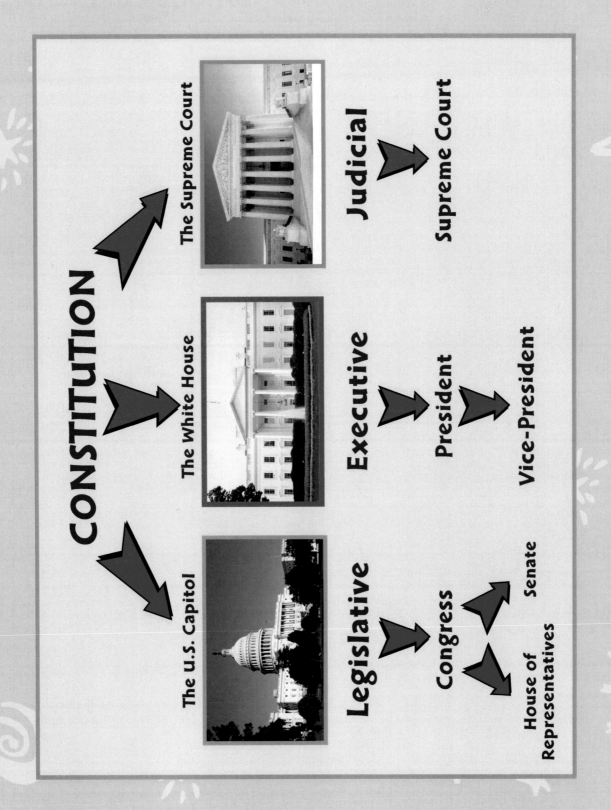

The U.S. Capitol Building
(Washington D.C.)

The Supreme Court
(Washington D.C.)

The White House
(Washington D.C.)

Constitution of the United States – Page 1

Publication Listing

• • • • • • • • • • • • • • • •

Ask Your Dealer About Our Complete Line

SOCIAL STUDIES - Software

ITEM #	TITLE
	MAPPING SKILLS SERIES
CC7770	Grades PK-2 Mapping Skills with Google Earth
CC7771	Grades 3-5 Mapping Skills with Google Earth
CC7772	Grades 6-8 Mapping Skills with Google Earth
CC7773	Grades PK-8 Mapping Skills with Google Earth Big Box

SOCIAL STUDIES - Books

	MAPPING SKILLS SERIES
CC5786	Grades PK-2 Mapping Skills with Google Earth
CC5787	Grades 3-5 Mapping Skills with Google Earth
CC5788	Grades 6-8 Mapping Skills with Google Earth
CC5789	Grades PK-8 Mapping Skills with Google Earth Big Book
	NORTH AMERICAN GOVERNMENTS SERIES
CC5757	American Government
CC5758	Canadian Government
CC5759	Mexican Government
CC5760	Governments of North America Big Book
	WORLD GOVERNMENTS SERIES
CC5761	World Political Leaders
CC5762	World Electoral Processes
CC5763	Capitalism vs. Communism
CC5777	World Politics Big Book
	WORLD CONFLICT SERIES
CC5511	American Revolutionary War
CC5500	American Civil War
CC5512	American Wars Big Book
CC5501	World War I
CC5502	World War II
CC5503	World Wars I & II Big Book
CC5505	Korean War
CC5506	Vietnam War
CC5507	Korean & Vietnam Wars Big Book
CC5508	Persian Gulf War (1990-1991)
CC5509	Iraq War (2003-2010)
CC5510	Gulf Wars Big Book
	WORLD CONTINENTS SERIES
CC5750	North America
CC5751	South America
CC5768	The Americas Big Book
CC5752	Europe
CC5753	Africa
CC5754	Asia
CC5755	Australia
CC5756	Antarctica
	WORLD CONNECTIONS SERIES
CC5782	Culture, Society & Globalization
CC5783	Economy & Globalization
CC5784	Technology & Globalization
CC5785	Globalization Big Book

REGULAR & REMEDIAL EDUCATION

• • • • • • • • • • • • • • •

Reading Level 3-4 Grades 5-8

ENVIRONMENTAL STUDIES - Software

ITEM #	TITLE
	CLIMATE CHANGE SERIES
CC7747	Global Warming: Causes Grades 3-8
CC7748	Global Warming: Effects Grades 3-8
CC7749	Global Warming: Reduction Grades 3-8
CC7750	Global Warming Big Box Grades 3-8

ENVIRONMENTAL STUDIES - Books

	MANAGING OUR WASTE SERIES
CC5764	Waste: At the Source
CC5765	Prevention, Recycling & Conservation
CC5766	Waste: The Global View
CC5767	Waste Management Big Book
	CLIMATE CHANGE SERIES
CC5769	Global Warming: Causes
CC5770	Global Warming: Effects
CC5771	Global Warming: Reduction
CC5772	Global Warming Big Book
	GLOBAL WATER SERIES
CC5773	Conservation: Fresh Water Resources
CC5774	Conservation: Ocean Water Resources
CC5775	Conservation: Waterway Habitats Resources
CC5776	Water Conservation Big Book
	CARBON FOOTPRINT SERIES
CC5778	Reducing Your Own Carbon Footprint
CC5779	Reducing Your School's Carbon Footprint
CC5780	Reducing Your Community's Carbon Footprint
CC5781	Carbon Footprint Big Book

SCIENCE - Software

ITEM #	TITLE
	SPACE AND BEYOND SERIES
CC7557	Solar System Grades 5-8
CC7558	Galaxies & the Universe Grades 5-8
CC7559	Space Travel & Technology Grades 5-8
CC7560	Space Big Box Grades 5-8
	HUMAN BODY SERIES
CC7549	Cells, Skeletal & Muscular Systems Grades 5-8
CC7550	Senses, Nervous & Respiratory Systems Grades 5-8
CC7551	Circulatory, Digestive & Reproductive Systems Grades 5-8
CC7552	Human Body Big Box Grades 5-8
	FORCE, MOTION & SIMPLE MACHINES SERIES
CC7553	Force Grades 3-8
CC7554	Motion Grades 3-8
CC7555	Simple Machines Grades 3-8
CC7556	Force, Motion & Simple Machines Big Box Grades 3-8

SCIENCE - Books

	ECOLOGY & THE ENVIRONMENT SERIES
CC4500	Ecosystems
CC4501	Classification & Adaptation
CC4502	Cells
CC4503	Ecology & The Environment Big Book
	MATTER & ENERGY SERIES
CC4504	Properties of Matter
CC4505	Atoms, Molecules & Elements
CC4506	Energy
CC4507	The Nature of Matter Big Book
	FORCE & MOTION SERIES
CC4508	Force
CC4509	Motion
CC4510	Simple Machines
CC4511	Force, Motion & Simple Machines Big Book
	SPACE & BEYOND SERIES
CC4512	Solar System
CC4513	Galaxies & The Universe
CC4514	Travel & Technology
CC4515	Space Big Book
	HUMAN BODY SERIES
CC4516	Cells, Skeletal & Muscular Systems
CC4517	Nervous, Senses & Respiratory Systems
CC4518	Circulatory, Digestive & Reproductive Systems
CC4519	Human Body Big Book

VISIT:

www.CLASSROOM COMPLETE PRESS.com

To view sample pages from each book

COMMON CORE

LITERATURE KITS™- Books

ITEM #	TITLE
	GRADES 1-2
CC2100	Curious George (H. A. Rey)
CC2101	Paper Bag Princess (Robert N. Munsch)
CC2102	Stone Soup (Marcia Brown)
CC2103	The Very Hungry Caterpillar (Eric Carle)
CC2104	Where the Wild Things Are (Maurice Sendak)
	GRADES 3-4
CC2300	Babe: The Gallant Pig (Dick King-Smith)
CC2301	Because of Winn-Dixie (Kate DiCamillo)
CC2302	The Tale of Despereaux (Kate DiCamillo)
CC2303	James and the Giant Peach (Roald Dahl)
CC2304	Ramona Quimby, Age 8 (Beverly Cleary)
CC2305	The Mouse and the Motorcycle (Beverly Cleary)
CC2306	Charlotte's Web (E.B. White)
CC2307	Owls in the Family (Farley Mowat)
CC2308	Sarah, Plain and Tall (Patricia MacLachlan)
CC2309	Matilda (Roald Dahl)
CC2310	Charlie & The Chocolate Factory (Roald Dahl)
CC2311	Frindle (Andrew Clements)
CC2312	M.C. Higgins, the Great (Virginia Hamilton)
CC2313	The Family Under The Bridge (N.S. Carlson)
CC2314	The Hundred Penny Box (Sharon Mathis)
CC2315	Cricket in Times Square (George Selden)
	GRADES 5-6
CC2500	Black Beauty (Anna Sewell)
CC2501	Bridge to Terabithia (Katherine Paterson)
CC2502	Bud, Not Buddy (Christopher Paul Curtis)
CC2503	The Egypt Game (Zilpha Keatley Snyder)
CC2504	The Great Gilly Hopkins (Katherine Paterson)
CC2505	Holes (Louis Sachar)
CC2506	Number the Stars (Lois Lowry)
CC2507	The Sign of the Beaver (E.G. Speare)
CC2508	The Whipping Boy (Sid Fleischman)
CC2509	Island of the Blue Dolphins (Scott O'Dell)
CC2510	Underground to Canada (Barbara Smucker)
CC2511	Loser (Jerry Spinelli)
CC2512	The Higher Power of Lucky (Susan Patron)
CC2513	Kira-Kira (Cynthia Kadohata)
CC2514	Dear Mr. Henshaw (Beverly Cleary)
CC2515	The Summer of the Swans (Betsy Byars)
CC2516	Shiloh (Phyllis Reynolds Naylor)
CC2517	A Single Shard (Linda Sue Park)
CC2518	Hoot (Carl Hiaasen)
CC2519	Hatchet (Gary Paulsen)
CC2520	The Giver (Lois Lowry)
CC2521	The Graveyard Book (Neil Gaiman)
CC2522	The View From Saturday (E.L Konigsburg)
CC2523	Hattie Big Sky (Kirby Larson)
CC2524	When You Reach Me (Rebecca Stead)
CC2525	Criss Cross (Lynne Rae Perkins)
CC2526	A Year Down Yonder (Richard Peak)
	GRADES 7-8
CC2700	Cheaper by the Dozen (Frank B. Gilbreth)
CC2701	The Miracle Worker (William Gibson)
CC2702	The Red Pony (John Steinbeck)
CC2703	Treasure Island (Robert Louis Stevenson)
CC2704	Romeo & Juliet (William Shakespeare)
CC2705	Crispin: The Cross of Lead (Avi)

LITERATURE KITS™- Books

ITEM #	TITLE
	GRADES 9-12
CC2001	To Kill A Mockingbird (Harper Lee)
CC2002	Angela's Ashes (Frank McCourt)
CC2003	The Grapes of Wrath (John Steinbeck)
CC2004	The Good Earth (Pearl S. Buck)
CC2005	The Road (Cormac McCarthy)
CC2006	The Old Man and the Sea (Ernest Hemingway)
CC2007	Lord of the Flies (William Golding)
CC2008	The Color Purple (Alice Walker)
CC2009	The Outsiders (S.E. Hinton)
CC2010	Hamlet (William Shakespeare)

LANGUAGE ARTS - Software

ITEM #	TITLE
	WORD FAMILIES SERIES
CC7112	Word Families - Short Vowels Grades PK-2
CC7113	Word Families - Long Vowels Grades PK-2
CC7114	Word Families - Vowels Big Box Grades PK-2
	SIGHT & PICTURE WORDS SERIES
CC7100	High Frequency Sight Words Grades PK-2
CC7101	High Frequency Picture Words Grades PK-2
CC7102	Sight & Picture Words Big Box Grades PK-2
	WRITING SKILLS SERIES
CC7104	How to Write a Paragraph Grades 5-8
CC7105	How to Write a Book Report Grades 5-8
CC7106	How to Write an Essay Grades 5-8
CC7107	Master Writing Big Box Grades 5-8
	READING SKILLS SERIES
CC7108	Reading Comprehension Grades 3-8
CC7109	Literary Devices Grades 3-8
CC7110	Critical Thinking Grades 3-8
CC7111	Master Reading Big Box Grades 3-8

LANGUAGE ARTS - Books

ITEM #	TITLE
	WORD FAMILIES SERIES
CC1110	Word Families - Short Vowels Grades PK-1
CC1111	Word Families - Long Vowels Grades PK-1
CC1112	Word Families - Vowels Big Book Grades K-1
	SIGHT & PICTURE WORDS SERIES
CC1113	High Frequency Sight Words Grades PK-1
CC1114	High Frequency Picture Words Grades PK-1
CC1115	Sight & Picture Words Big Book Grades PK-1
	WRITING SKILLS SERIES
CC1100	How to Write a Paragraph Grades 5-8
CC1101	How to Write a Book Report Grades 5-8
CC1102	How to Write an Essay Grades 5-8
CC1103	Master Writing Big Book Grades 5-8
	READING SKILLS SERIES
CC7108	Reading Comprehension Grades 5-8
CC7109	Literary Devices Grades 5-8
CC7110	Critical Thinking Grades 5-8
CC7111	Master Reading Big Book Grades 5-8
	READING RESPONSE FORMS SERIES
CC1106	Reading Response Forms: Grades 1-2
CC1107	Reading Response Forms: Grades 3-4
CC1108	Reading Response Forms: Grades 5-6
CC1109	Reading Response Forms Big Book: Grades 1-6

MATHEMATICS - Software

ITEM #	TITLE
	PRINCIPLES & STANDARDS OF MATH SERIES
CC7315	Grades PK-2 Five Strands of Math Big Box
CC7316	Grades 3-5 Five Strands of Math Big Box
CC7317	Grades 6-8 Five Strands of Math Big Box

MATHEMATICS - Books

ITEM #	TITLE
	PRINCIPLES & STANDARDS OF MATH SERIES
CC3100	Grades PK-2 Number & Operations Task Sheets
CC3101	Grades PK-2 Algebra Task Sheets
CC3102	Grades PK-2 Geometry Task Sheets
CC3103	Grades PK-2 Measurement Task Sheets
CC3104	Grades PK-2 Data Analysis & Probability Task Sheets
CC3105	Grades PK-2 Five Strands of Math Big Book Task Sheets
CC3106	Grades 3-5 Number & Operations Task Sheets
CC3107	Grades 3-5 Algebra Task Sheets
CC3108	Grades 3-5 Geometry Task Sheets
CC3109	Grades 3-5 Measurement Task Sheets
CC3110	Grades 3-5 Data Analysis & Probability Task Sheets
CC3111	Grades 3-5 Five Strands of Math Big Book Task Sheets
CC3112	Grades 6-8 Number & Operations Task Sheets
CC3113	Grades 6-8 Algebra Task Sheets
CC3114	Grades 6-8 Geometry Task Sheets
CC3115	Grades 6-8 Measurement Task Sheets
CC3116	Grades 6-8 Data Analysis & Probability Task Sheets
CC3117	Grades 6-8 Five Strands of Math Big Book Task Sheets
	PRINCIPLES & STANDARDS OF MATH SERIES
CC3200	Grades PK-2 Number & Operations Drill Sheets
CC3201	Grades PK-2 Algebra Drill Sheets
CC3202	Grades PK-2 Geometry Drill Sheets
CC3203	Grades PK-2 Measurement Drill Sheets
CC3204	Grades PK-2 Data Analysis & Probability Drill Sheets
CC3205	Grades PK-2 Five Strands of Math Big Book Drill Sheets
CC3206	Grades 3-5 Number & Operations Drill Sheets
CC3207	Grades 3-5 Algebra Drill Sheets
CC3208	Grades 3-5 Geometry Drill Sheets
CC3209	Grades 3-5 Measurement Drill Sheets
CC3210	Grades 3-5 Data Analysis & Probability Drill Sheets
CC3211	Grades 3-5 Five Strands of Math Big Book Drill Sheets
CC3212	Grades 6-8 Number & Operations Drill Sheets
CC3213	Grades 6-8 Algebra Drill Sheets
CC3214	Grades 6-8 Geometry Drill Sheets
CC3215	Grades 6-8 Measurement Drill Sheets
CC3216	Grades 6-8 Data Analysis & Probability Drill Sheets
CC3217	Grades 6-8 Five Strands of Math Big Book Drill Sheets
	PRINCIPLES & STANDARDS OF MATH SERIES
CC3300	Grades PK-2 Number & Operations Task & Drill Sheets
CC3301	Grades PK-2 Algebra Task & Drill Sheets
CC3302	Grades PK-2 Geometry Task & Drill Sheets
CC3303	Grades PK-2 Measurement Task & Drill Sheets
CC3304	Grades PK-2 Data Analysis & Probability Task & Drills
CC3306	Grades 3-5 Number & Operations Task & Drill Sheets
CC3307	Grades 3-5 Algebra Task & Drill Sheets
CC3308	Grades 3-5 Geometry Task & Drill Sheets
CC3309	Grades 3-5 Measurement Task & Drill Sheets
CC3310	Grades 3-5 Data Analysis & Probability Task & Drills
CC3312	Grades 6-8 Number & Operations Task & Drill Sheets
CC3313	Grades 6-8 Algebra Task & Drill Sheets
CC3314	Grades 6-8 Geometry Task & Drill Sheets
CC3315	Grades 6-8 Measurement Task & Drill Sheets
CC3316	Grades 6-8 Data Analysis & Probability Task & Drills